Black Cotton

The Harvesting of Our Youth

By

Vincent D. Lewis

The Harvesting of Our Youth

Black Cotton

Black Cotton

The Harvesting of Our Youth

Black Cotton

The Harvesting of Our Youth

TABLE OF CONTENTS

Black Cotton

The Harvesting of Our Youth

"The time for justice, the time for freedom, the time for equality, is always right now" (Washington, 2007).

Black Cotton

Acknowledgments

I owe a deep debt of gratitude to the many people who have supported the vision and process of writing this book. Every one of them deserves to be personally acknowledged for his or her contribution.

Dorothy Jones-Love, my mother, is the reason I am alive to write this book. She supported me unconditionally throughout my turbulent youth and beyond. As with many mothers, she raised her children amidst almost impossible odds. With an unwavering belief in God and the unity of our family, my mother has been and will always be my hero.

Lee David Lewis, my father, his life has taught me many hard but valuable lessons, and for my inheriting his ability to dream.

Katherine Denise Lewis, my wife, has been an inspiration to me during this process. As Director of an Intensive Adolescent Boy's Treatment program in

Black Cotton

The Harvesting of Our Youth

Augusta, Georgia, she has a real gift for reaching at risk youth. Her insight and practical experience has proven to be invaluable.

Malcolm King Lewis, my youngest son, is my little miracle that survived a premature birth on Dr. Martin Luther King Jr. Day. My love for him, his kind spirit and gentle nature is a constant reminder of why I wrote this book. I want to protect him and all other children from a corrupt system that is targeting their future.

Also, to my older sons **Vincent Lewis Jr., Daniel Lewis and Jamal Lewis,** I fight for their futures and pray for them daily.

Letasha Lewis, my sister, has always been a great inspiration to me. She and her two children **Christopher Lee Lewis and Emma Marie Lewis** are in my support network also. They make me laugh and keep me working to secure the future for their well being. As a Critical Care Nurse in Memphis, which is currently one of our nation's most violent cities, my sister all too often witnesses the end result of poverty and lack of hope in our communities. She has been a great source of information for this project.

$\mathbf{B}$lack Cotton

Southern New Hampshire University's School of Community Economic Development is where I received my Masters Degree in CED. I will be eternally grateful for the education and relationships that I acquired as a result of attending this great school. The wonderful professors and diverse group of students from around the world truly taught me the importance of fighting for social and economic justice.

To the men and women of God who fight this war daily. You have been such an inspiration to me. Countless trips to prisons, jails and street corners along with your willingness to mentor and provide real opportunity for our brothers and sisters returning from jails and prison, serves as the only promised land many of our people will ever know. Thank you for putting your faith into action. Thank you to the entire **Lewis and Jones Families** for their love and support throughout my life, especially my grandmothers, Nornee Lewis and Emma Jones, may they rest in peace.

To Tremmel – There is hope brother, hold on.

Black Cotton

Dr. Julian Bond

"The truth is there are no non-racial remedies for racial discrimination. In order to get beyond race, you have to go to race. To suggest racial neutrality as a remedy for racial discrimination is sophistry of the highest order" (Bond, 2007).

$\mathbf{B}$lack Cotton

The Harvesting of Our Youth

Introduction

This book is intended to shine a bright light on the suffering of young black males involved in the criminal justice system. Because this problem has many different roots, it is impossible to simply write about crime and incarceration rates. So I discuss various issues contributing to the weakening of the black community as a whole, which results in higher incarceration rates among black males.

Although race should not be a factor in our criminal justice system, it simply cannot be ignored. When discussing racial disparities in America, many people view it as the unnecessary opening of old wounds. Without discussing race it is impossible to truly understand how we went from being slaves in this country to find ourselves making up half of its 2,000,000 inmates. This is very troubling since we only make up 13% of the population.

I therefore confront this issue head on by discussing the lingering psychological effects of slavery and the resulting broken criminal justice system (Yuksel, 2001).

Black Cotton

The Harvesting of Our Youth

In addition, we can always find crooks with their hands in our pockets, getting paid from our social challenges. The mass incarceration of mostly black men is big business. American corporations, communities and even regions depend on prison beds remaining full to support their economies.

In the chapter titled "The Black Cotton Agenda", I offer solutions for fixing this broken system. I hope all who read this text will be inspired to make a meaningful contribution in the fight for reform in the American criminal justice system.

It has been said that the biggest trick the devil has ever played on mankind is to make us believe he does not exist. In many ways, those in power use the very same tactic to control our perception of justice. In recent years we have seen what many believe to be an unjust war, waged in the name of defending freedom. Now we see the profitable mass incarceration of our citizens, mostly black men, in the name of public safety.

When I was a little younger, my mother taught me many lessons about life. Many of these lessons I chose to challenge. She often said, "If you don't believe what I am telling you son, just live a little longer, and you will come to understand." Well, I have come to understand many things that she tried to teach me were right on target. One of those memorable lessons was that there is a little bit of bad in the best of us and a little bit of good in the worst of us. As I became older, my understanding of this lesson evolved into realizing that good and evil are both very real, and they exist in us all. In addition, this lesson taught me that every good lie has some truth to it, and because of this, the good in us wants to believe the lie.

This book attempts to get past the thin veneer of truth presented by our broken criminal justice system. I hope to expose the injustice behind it. This book is not an attempt to demonize our government or any particular race or religion. As I have stated earlier, I believe that every person has the capacity to do good or evil.

We must confront the issue of race because as the title suggests, black males are disproportionately affected by the injustice in the criminal justice system. There is a racial problem within the system and it must be confronted head on.

This book will also attempt to help us clearly understand how we got in this situation. I will provide some suggestions on how to fix the problem, or should I say, confront the evil.

Black Cotton

The Harvesting of Our Youth

Why Black Cotton? I thought the title was appropriate for the situation we find ourselves in today. The title suggests that Americans once relied on black people to slave in their cotton fields, carrying out the injustice of state-sanctioned pain, human suffering, and servitude for the profits enjoyed by plantation owners. Now in modern times we see the same justification for the mass incarceration of mostly black males by our so-called criminal justice system. The descendants of the black folks, who used to pick cotton in America, particularly black men, have now become the product picked off the streets. This black cotton picking happens mostly in our urban gardens. Similar to the cotton gin, which was invented to separate the seed from the cotton, prisons managed and owned by descendants of slave owners are separating large numbers of black men from their seed, their children. Without being able to remain attached to their seed, black men become breeders of the next generation of black cotton. Many children of incarcerated black men are suffering because their fathers are not there to prevent them from falling on the same fertile ground of our urban streets.

A Manageable Crop

According to Douglas Egerton, "In many ways, cotton was the perfect crop for slave labor to produce. Unlike cereal crops, it didn't grow very high. In short, workers could always be observed by the overseers. It was perfect for the gang style of labor organization." The parallels to the current situation are sobering when you think about it.

Just as the cotton crop was perfect for the overseers, urban youth provide the same type of manageability for the modern overseers or officers. Because of poverty and lack of opportunity, many urban youth will not grow beyond their communities. They will never be allowed to attain the power that can challenge the injustice perpetrated by the prison industrial complex that is harvesting them for profit.

Gang style policing of our urban communities has become all too common in today's society. Even affluent black leaders find themselves being harassed by modern-day overseers.

Because of so called get tough on crime public safety mandates, lingering racism among some, open flood gates of international narcotics in poor communities and poverty, these peacekeepers profile black and brown people with seemingly unbridled disregard for justice.

Black Cotton

The Harvesting of Our Youth

A Culture of Kidnapping

I really want to be clear about what's truly happening in America today concerning this issue. We are witnessing the legal kidnapping of our children. Critics may say that this statement is really strong and may not reflect the reality of what is actually happening. I would ask, whose reality are they referring to? The fact is, many black mothers and grandmothers await their children to come home from school or a trip to the corner store, praying they don't get locked up or worse. This is because of the out-of-control crime rate and the injustice perpetrated by the police paid to protect citizens.

In urban communities, we hear story after story of cops shooting unarmed black youth or beating them unmercifully for no apparent reason. For black people, who have experienced so many great injustices in this country, this experience feels painfully familiar.

During slavery, many blacks escaped to the North to cities like Philadelphia, where they could be free. Slave owners in the South employed bounty hunters to bring escaped blacks back. In many cases, these so-called bounty hunters also kidnapped free black children from schools and other places. These bounty hunters then sold the children into slavery.

Black Cotton

The Harvesting of Our Youth

According to Emma Lapsansky, professor of history at Haverford College, "Anybody who didn't have proof of freedom could be snatched up and taken. Or anybody who did have it could be snatched up, papers destroyed, and you could be taken off to the South." Children who should have felt safe in their country had to worry about those in power snatching them off the streets (Lapsansky, n.d.).

Where are our values?

To further understand this culture of kidnapping; we have to confront serious questions about so-called American values. The questions I would ask the folks who seem to have the strongest opinion about this, namely the Christian conservative groups and organizations, are as follows:

1. What is it about the American-values champions that make them turn a deaf ear to the abuse and suffering of young black and brown males in this country?
2. Why aren't these value peddlers using their influence to end police brutality and racial profiling?
3. As a Christian, I often feel like my brothers and sisters in Christ are faking it. I mean, come on,

The Harvesting of Our Youth

aren't we supposed to care for the poor and the powerless?

I am sure someone will come up with a biblical justification for the church not being at the forefront of social and political outrage on these issues, but I am equally certain that they would be wrong.

We cannot afford to live in pretense concerning issues that threaten our very existence. Therefore, I want to make my position clear as it relates to the church.

The church as an institution stands for the best of what mankind has to offer and deserves respect and care when discussed; however, it can be said that the church has also supported or ignored some of the greatest human-rights violations in history. For example, slavery, lynching, and raping of a people, post-slavery oppression, apartheid, the slaughter of Native Americans, abuse and neglect of Hurricane Katrina victims, and much more.

If the church were true to its creed, it would have to shout and protest these issues unto the highest levels of our government; nevertheless, we hear little more than a whisper from my brothers and sisters.

Maybe it's because they are afraid.

***B**lack Cotton*

The Harvesting of Our Youth

In many of our liberal African American churches, we hear the same deafening silence. Maybe it stems from fear of losing their members, money, or tax status.

The church seems to have lost its passion for social justice and the willingness to wage battle outside its own walls. The long fight for justice seems to have left very few standing. Who can the leaders of yesterday turn the "torch light of justice" over to? This seems like an impossible task if black youth are being harvested while white youth are going to Harvard.

While fighting for justice during civil rights movement, we saw young and old walk side by side or sit cell by cell if necessary. Because of the zeal of the young, the patients and wisdom of the old, we have seen great changes in our country. We saw young leaders rise up from the streets of injustice like the Black Panther Party and others.

Where are these young activists today?

Why aren't church leaders encouraging the youth to organize against the prison industrial complex?

Black Cotton

The Harvesting of Our Youth

Are we simply to encourage the youth to come to church, pay their tithes and offerings, participate in praise, worship and bible study?

It appears that many people in the black community feel that we have outgrown the need for leaders. Well, not only have we not outgrown the need for leaders, we need them more than ever.

Let's consider why the church must begin aggressively encouraging the youth to appropriately do battle against the prison industrial complex.

Hundreds of thousands of our young men are being used as slaves in our prisons. Many of them locked up for nonviolent crimes and some falsely accused altogether. They are literally sold to prisons that are publicly traded corporations. These privately owned prison companies contract with state or federal governments to house inmates at a reduced cost, thereby saving the government money.

Now that it has become profitable to lock people up, the overseers/officers harvest them from the most fertile ground for crime, the inner city.

Black Cotton

The Harvesting of Our Youth

So I respectfully say to all of you who do not think we need leaders; we need them more than ever. We need men and women both young and old with the courage to go from state to state and way down into the heart of our land, the capital, and tell our so-called public servants, **"Let our people go!"**

Black Cotton

Dr. Cornel West

"No other people in the modern world have had such unprecedented levels of unregulated violence against them. Psychic violence taught to hate ourselves and told we have the wrong hips and lips and noses and hair texture and skin pigmentation. Physical violence, slavery, Jim Crow, lynching, police brutality"(West, 2001).

Effects of Slavery

There have been many books written about slavery, and I believe most of America is at least familiar with the subject. I think most Americans, black, white, or otherwise, would agree that it was a terrible part of our history. Where most of these opinions begin to part company is when those negatively affected by slavery, namely black folks, begin to speak up about the injustice of that time and the lingering effects thereof.

The psychological, social, and economic effects of slavery on black and white America can't be denied.

$\mathbf{B}$lack Cotton

The Harvesting of Our Youth

Issues to consider when thinking about the effects of slavery:

- Blacks and whites were psychologically damaged by slavery.
- Slavery discouraged independent judgment and self-reliance in slaves.
- Slaves led a harsh lifestyle and were not allowed to question anything.
- Slave owners enjoyed the use of brute force with slaves.
- Slave owners took advantage of black women.
- Slave owners considered the breeding of women for profit as just another part of business.
- Conditions on slave-trade ships were horrible enough to cause severe psychological trauma that has continued in part for generations.

The psychological damage is clear and has been passed down from generation to generation. Many whites have passed on their false sense of superiority, and many blacks have inherited the psychological trauma inflicted on their ancestors. Many generations of sons and daughters of former slaves and slave owners have come and gone. Although the world's knowledge about genetics, psychology, and sociology has greatly

---

increased, the deeply rooted effects of slavery still glare through.

The psychological effects have caused some of the most violent revolts in this country. The false sense of security and superiority has led many whites to act in ways that are not in their long-term best interest.

Whites who still hold onto this way of thinking have been blinded by a false reality. History has shown time and time again that oppressed people will eventually rise up against their oppressors.

Black Cotton

Minister Louis Farrakhan

"If we don't make earnest moves toward real solutions, then each day we move one day closer to revolution and anarchy in this country. This is the sad, and yet potentially joyous, state of America" (Farrakhan, 1993).

Black Cotton

The Harvesting of Our Youth

Examples of historic revolts:

Gabriel Prosser 1776-1800

The first major slave revolt in the South was led by a twenty-four-year-old slave named Gabriel Prosser. All the major slave revolts in the South were led by people like Prosser. They were deeply rooted Christians and were fired by religious indignation against slavery. Prosser was the first. In 1800, he began to lay plans to take the city of Richmond, Virginia, by force. He planned to invade Richmond, attack the armory, and arm his rebel slaves. By August 1800, he had nearly a thousand slaves enlisted and had stored up an arsenal of weapons. On the day of his revolt, with more than a thousand followers ready to attack Richmond, the bridges into the city were destroyed in a flood. He was betrayed by two followers, and the state militia attacked him the next day. He and many of his followers were hanged. Although Prosser's revolt ended in defeat, it terrified slave owners throughout the South. Prosser had come very close to taking Richmond. If he had not been betrayed, and if the bridges had not washed out, it is almost certain that he would have successfully taken the city of Richmond with his slave followers. Prosser's revolt was the closest America came to a revolution on the same scale as that in Haiti (Hooker, 1996).

Black Cotton

The Harvesting of Our Youth

Denmark Vesey 1767-1822

Denmark Vesey, like so many other African-American leaders of the nineteenth century, came from the "upper class" of slaves: the engineers and craftspeople who were given a high degree of independence and self-actualization, as opposed to field workers or house slaves. He purchased his own freedom and settled down as a carpenter in Charleston, South Carolina.

Despite the surface placidity of his free life, he was fired with anger over slavery and the situation of black slaves. Throughout his entire free existence, he planned and thought about freeing his fellow slaves. He was so full of anger that companions say that he could not even remain in the presence of a European-American (Hooker, 1996).

Like Prosser, Vesey was also deeply inspired by Christianity, in particular, the Old Testament. An integral aspect of slave and free Christianity was its emphasis on the delivery of the "children of Israel" from bondage in Egypt. This story was perhaps the most powerful religious and cultural influence on the world view of nineteenth century Americans. While most historians stress the passive nature of the Israelite deliverance, that deliverance was also yoked to the Israelite invasion of the land of Canaan. While this

---

Black Cotton

---

invasion was barely successful, the Old Testament books telling the history of the Canaan occupation and its aftermath are ruthlessly violent and present a warrior god with no mercy towards non-Israelites. All evidence we have suggests that slaves understood that these two events were connected and that deliverance along Israelite lines would be bought with human blood. Vesey, who went around quoting biblical texts to slaves to inspire them to revolt, particularly loved to quote Yahweh's instructions to Joshua when he demands that Joshua kill every occupant of the cities of Canaan including women and children (Hooker, 1996).

 His task, as he saw it, was to incite slaves into revolt. In 1821, that focus changed dramatically and he began to organize his own revolt. He organized a working group of lieutenants that included Gullah Jack, a sorcerer considered absolutely invulnerable and Peter Poyas who was one of the great military and organizational geniuses of the early nineteenth century. Poyas organized the revolt into separate cells under individual leaders. Only the leaders knew the plot; if any slave betrayed the plot, they would only betray their one cell. By 1822, almost all the slaves in the plantations surrounding Charleston had joined the revolt. His and Poyas's plan was brilliantly simple. The rebels would all station themselves at the doors of European-Americans and, late at night, a group of rebels would start a major fire. When the men came out their doors, the rebels would kill them with axes, picks, or guns. They would then enter the houses and kill all the occupants. Like Prosser's revolt, they almost won. They were betrayed early in the game, but the cell structure prevented officials from finding out the plot itself or identifying any of the leaders. It was only the day before that a slave, who knew the entire plot, betrayed Vesey. He and his co-leaders were hung, but only one confessed (Hooker, 1996).

Nat Turner 1800-1831

Vesey's revolt was immensely frightening to southern slave-owners. Not only was it difficult to crack the plot, despite the fact that thousands of slaves were involved, but the sheer thoroughness of the violence planned chilled the hearts of even the most confident slave owners. That so many slaves would be willing to exterminate any and all European Americans regardless of gender or age brought home the depth of feeling, anger, and resistance that surrounded slave owners all day long (Hooker, 1996).

Black Cotton

The Harvesting of Our Youth

Neither Prosser's nor Vesey's rebellions actually succeeded; despite their fear, European-Americans believed that, in the end, God had protected them. This would all change, however, when a man that slaves simply called Prophet, Nat Turner, led a short revolt in which God did not protect slave owners (Hooker, 1996). Turner, like Vesey, was from the "upper class" of slaves. He had grown up deeply hating slavery; his mother, an African, so hated slavery that she tried to kill him when he was born in 1800 to prevent him from living the life of a slave. He, too, was religious, in fact, far more than Vesey and Prosser. His Christianity was a religion of visions and mystical experience. By the time he was a young man, Turner had become unofficially the major religious leader in Southampton, a County in Virginia. Unlike Vesey, Turner's Christianity emphasized not the Israelite deliverance, but the latter days of Christ in Jerusalem and the apocalyptic promise of a New Jerusalem. His rhetoric had a place as well as a spiritual meaning: Jerusalem, Virginia, which lay nearby.

All his disciples, seven of them, were fired up by anger and religious passion. One had been so abused by his master that he was covered with scars. On the appointed night on Sunday, they left Turner's house and entered the house of his master where, with only one hatchet and one broadax between them, they executed all the

The Harvesting of Our Youth

members, including two teens, with the exception of an infant. They then moved from house to house throughout the night and executed every European-American they could find with the exception of a white family that owned no slaves; Will chopped up his master and his wife so passionately that Turner called him "Will the Executioner." As they went from house to house they gathered slaves and weapons. By Monday, they were approaching Jerusalem but were turned back by a regiment of European-Americans. Turner dug a cave and went into hiding, but when troops arrived they scoured the countryside and executed slaves by the hundred. Turner, however, was never caught for over two months; during all this time, Virginians were seized with panic. Hundred fled the county and many left the state for good. Turner, however, was eventually captured and hung. This was the last straw; from this point onwards, no slave owner lived comfortably with slavery now that they understood the anger, the resistance, and the vengeance that boiled beneath the burden of slavery (Hooker, 1996).

History records as many as 250 slave uprisings. Many revolts were small and quickly crushed, but the revolts still struck fear in the hearts of slave owners. The result was the enactment of stricter laws against slaves. Punishment became increasingly harsh, and because these revolts were led by mostly black men, whites made it a practice to keep the punishment both psychological and physically demoralizing as much as possible (Bird, 2005).

Today the sons of former slave owners have become very efficient in keeping down any significant uprising among the sons of former slaves. Because of the psychological effects of slavery there are systems built in our government to keep the black male in invisible bondage. Unfortunately, this invisible captivity often translates into physical incarceration.

In the chapters called The Crop and The Gin, we will deal with the issue of the mass incarceration of black men. I think any reasonable person would agree, that the fact that 50% of black men between the ages eighteen and thirty-five, being negatively involved with the criminal justice system, is a tragedy. I believe that this problem is a social epidemic that threatens the future of black America. This crisis is a direct result of the psychological effects of slavery and a modern method of controlling the spirit and strength of young black males.

Black Cotton

The Harvesting of Our Youth

Economics of Slavery

The success of many corporations in America can be directly attributed to slavery.

The modern-day fight for reparations has rightly targeted American corporations that were built on the backs of black folks but that do not benefit them directly today. The wealth controlled by these corporations is staggering. Billions upon billions of dollars are being made each year with no real stake in black communities. This is significant on many levels. Let's consider the argument of many white Americans today that they aren't responsible for what their ancestors did. Let's also consider their other argument that blacks have no right to the massive capital generated by corporations built on the backs of their slave ancestors. Both these arguments simply deflate under the light of examination. In the real world we benefit from the wealth of our ancestors both directly and indirectly. When your racial group controls the capital in a nation, your group controls the nation. Groups also invest that capital in communities where they have kinship and support charities that are racially specific to them. Conversely, blacks are at a disadvantage for investment and support for their charities. In addition, they do not control the capital their ancestors created. Simply put, the wealth of the nation can be directly attributed to slave labor, and those who

$\mathbf{B}$lack Cotton

The Harvesting of Our Youth

should benefit from the labor of their ancestors do not. According to Piette, 2005, in an article on workers.org, Wachovia bank admits to slave profits. Executives at Wachovia Bank disclosed in a June 2, 2005 report that the bank's predecessor institutions—the Bank of Charleston, S.C., and the Georgia Railroad and Banking Company—"owned" at least 162 enslaved Africans and accepted 529 more as collateral on loans. The article goes on to state; "It also revealed that war financier Robert Morris—a founder of a forerunner institution, Bank of North America—used profits from the slave trade to start Wachovia in 1781," and the Bank of Charleston provided financial assistance to the Confederate government throughout the Civil War. The admission by the North-Carolina-based Wachovia, the country's fourth-largest bank, follows similar disclosures by Lehman Brothers; J.P. Morgan Chase and Co., which is parent company of Bank One; and the Savings Bank of Baltimore, which is part of the Wachovia network. Like Wachovia, J. P. Morgan Chase initially disavowed ties to slavery. Eventually, Morgan executives were forced to acknowledge that two predecessor banks accepted 13,000 enslaved Africans as collateral, taking "ownership" of 1,250 of them, when loans defaulted. There were more than four million enslaved Africans in the United States in 1865 when

Black Cotton

slavery was abolished with ratification of the Thirteenth Amendment to the Constitution.

The legacy of slavery, however, continues to be felt today. Major struggles for reparations are being waged, which includes demands for federal reparations legislation. There are also lawsuits seeking billions of dollars from such companies as R.J. Reynolds, Aetna, and CSX Corporation for the descendants of enslaved Africans. The disclosures by these major banking institutions were made under pressure from the cities of Chicago, Philadelphia, Los Angeles, Detroit, and Richmond, Virginia. These cities passed ordinances calling on city contractors to reveal any history of making money from slavery (Brooks, 1996).

The Beneficiaries

Roy Brooks, a law professor at San Diego University, suggests we imagine a 400-year poker game between black and white people. The white player finally admits cheating and agrees to call a new, fair game. "Well, that's great," says the black player, "but what are you going to do with all the chips you've won?" The white player says he will keep them for the next generation of white players (Brooks, 1996).

Black Cotton

The Harvesting of Our Youth

As simple as this may sound, it gets very complicated when the players are the citizens of the United States. With a myriad of competing agendas and ideas among black folks and a system designed from its inception to oppose those agendas and ideas. It becomes a very challenging task to realize anything that resembles real justice.

Although slavery is history and those negatively affected by it are trapped in a perpetual state of complaining, the fact remains that it happened and will not fade into history, as many have hoped. In fact, it would be almost reasonable to let the sins of the past simply fade into time if there were not so much pain and residual injustice that still remains today. Injustices such as the mass incarceration of young black males for nonviolent offenses and the intentional mis-education of young black youth about the significance of their history are constant reminders.

The systematic discrediting, degrading, and even slaughtering of leaders who would aid black folks and the poor all contribute to mistrust and lack of faith in our nation and its criminal justice system.

Conversely, the descendants of slave owners have benefited from the generational wealth and prosperity

Black Cotton

passed down to them. I realize that there was then and there are now many poor whites in America. But even they have the promise of their ancestors that makes them feel their whiteness has value. This creates the paradox that can only be described as schizoid of the soul. This schizoid condition makes poor whites support those who oppress them, namely wealthy white politicians supporting big corporations.

Despite the apparent lack of genuine concern for them from those they regularly vote for in Washington, many poor whites feel bound by age old generational prejudices against minorities and so-called liberals who could be their natural allies in the fight for real social and economic justice.

Black Cotton

Eldridge Cleaver

"When Martin Luther King was turning towards the economic arena in Nashville supporting the strike of the garbage man, he was murdered. I applaud my country for the changes that we have undertaken in these areas of civil rights. But where the big problem still remains is with the economic system" (Cleaver, 1998).

Black Cotton

The Harvesting of Our Youth

Fact

As of June 30, 2007, the incarceration rate in state or federal prison or jail for men was 1,406 per 100,000 residents, for women 136 per 100,000 residents.

The rate for white men was 773 per 100,000, for black men 4,618 per 100,000, for Hispanic men 1,747 per 100,000.

The rate for white women was 95 per 100,000, for black women 348 per 100,000, and for Hispanic women 146 per 100,000 (Common Sense for Drug Policy , 2008).

The Harvesting of Our Youth

The Crop

Cotton should be planted in well-prepared seedbeds that are firm, warm, and moist. Planting should be based on soil temperature and the weather outlook for a month after planting. It is generally recommended that you plant only after soil temperatures at the eight-inch depth average a minimum of 60°F for ten days (temperature should be taken at 8 a.m.). Weather outlook is important because rain and cool temperatures following planting can slow germination and reduce growth.

The same factors that delay germination and seedling growth encourage seedling disease and insect problems. The first challenge encountered by the developing cotton plant is a seedling disease complex made up of one or more soil-borne fungi. You may know these seedling diseases by more familiar names: pythium, rhizoctonia, and thielaviopsis. Treating plant seed with fungicides often helps ward off seedling diseases (Deterling, 1982).

Black Cotton Crop Development

Black Cotton should be developed in well-prepared seedbeds of impoverished communities that are drug infested, have poor schools, and mostly single-parent households. Planting should be based on political climate, because the crop won't perform if the community has fiery political leadership. It is recommended that you attempt growing black cotton in a lukewarm political environment that consistently ignores the plight of young black males, a condition that serves as an appropriate level of social and economic discouragement for them and makes for a better crop. Political weather outlook is important, because the rain of discontentment among grassroots leaders may spark a movement to upset crop growth. Also, cool legal minds of civil-rights attorneys may be engaged to prevent further attempts to plant and grow black cotton.

The same factors that delay germination and seedling growth of black cotton encourages seedling health, education, and empowerment, which cause problems for crop production. The first challenge to developing black cotton is seedling fathering complex, caused by a responsible adult male in the home. This fathering

$\mathbf{B}$lack Cotton

complex is made up of one or more strong black men who grow tall and healthy in spite of previous black cotton development efforts. You may know seedling fathering factors by more familiar names: dad, uncle, and pastor. Treating black cotton seed with fungicides such as crack, heroin, and alcohol often helps seedlings to turn against the fathering complex.

Infant Mortality Disparity

Federal health officials warned in 1960 that for blacks the risk of dying before the age of one was twice that of whites. The current black infant mortality rate in America is still very high compared to whites. Lack of adequate healthcare and access to other vital resources has been linked to this problem. PBS has a series called "Unnatural Causes" that has a segment named "When the bough breaks" that establishes not only correlation between Blacks and low child birth weight but also causation with a link to racism (PBS, n.d.).

Black Cotton

The Harvesting of Our Youth

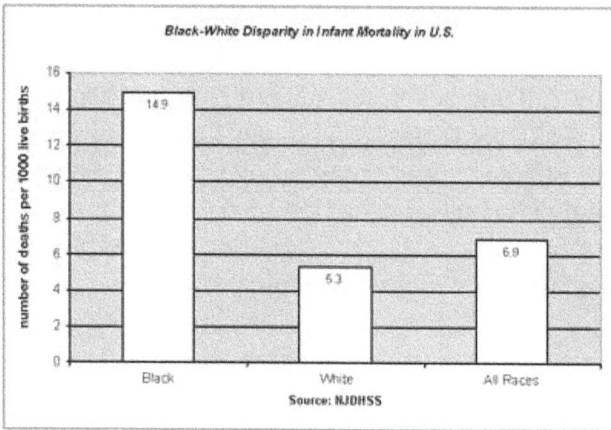

Black-White Disparity in Infant Mortality in U.S.

(Figure 3: 1996 Infant Mortality Rates in New Jersey)

The above chart shows a significant disparity in New Jersey in 1996, as reported by the New Jersey Department of Health and Senior Services. Similar stats can be found all across America. This tragedy is but one of a long list of social, political, economic, and spiritual issues that are threatening the existence of the black community. We survived kidnapping, confinement and inhumane conditions without an equal shot for survival, only to find that growing up in America will be a maze of injustice in which we have become a product for harvesting.

To truly understand how black males are seen as a product by state, federal, and private prisons, we need

Black Cotton

The Harvesting of Our Youth

only look at what it takes for these businesses to thrive. In any business you expect to make a reasonable profit, and in the prison business, more prisoners equal more profit. Private prison firms house and manage inmates through contracts with the state.

The problem with this setup is that once you make locking people up profitable, you unleash a beast with a hunger that continues to grow. Good old American greed, the byproduct of capitalism, will ensure that for-profit prisons will keep locking up prisoners for many years to come.

As with any good business, they plan ahead far into the future, so the private prison industry lobbies for stricter laws and longer sentencing.

Deeply rooted racism, which still exists in America, and disproportionately harsh laws that target black males virtually guarantee that prison firms will have a steady stream of product to count on.

What this equates to is a system that pays politicians to call for more arrests, and this responsibility ultimately trickles down to local police officers who have become the wage slaves who pick the new cotton, young black males.

Black Cotton

The Harvesting of Our Youth

Black males, the new crop for a criminal justice system run amok, are systematically targeted by law enforcement simply because it is easy to target them. They don't have the economic or political strength to defend against the often brutal and unjust system. When the prison industry sends a wave of cash out in the sea of career politicians, it calls for increases in public safety, and instead of targeting the real criminals, namely the private interests that support this injustice, politicians pass laws that allow officers to take the path of least resistance, incarcerating those who have less power to defend against the schemes of private-prison-industry investors.

In the beginning of this text I shared with you the reason I call this book *Black Cotton*. The parallels are profound among the commercial African slave trade, cotton production and harvesting and gang style policing of slaves and today's black cotton production and harvesting and gang style policing of black males. We see our young black men being killed or killing each other over mostly drug-related issues daily.

Today, I watched comedian Bill Cosby and Alvin F. Poussaint, M.D., of Harvard Medical School on CNN's *Larry King Show*. Cosby was shown a clip of himself speaking to a church group about the time the black community defended against terrorist attacks from the

KKK, but now we can't seem to see that the crack dealer is just as bad.

Also, Dr. Poussaint shared that in Baltimore there is currently a 75% high-school dropout rate among black males. In addition, there are 2,000,000 people currently in prison in America and more than 1,000,000 of them are black. The percentage of blacks in prison is made worse by the fact that blacks make up only about 13% of the nation. (Cosby, 2007).

Clearly, blacks are the ideal crop for the prison economy. The mass incarceration and self-destruction of our youth is now the most devastating situation we have ever faced. If we don't work to end this decline in our mental, physical, and spiritual wellbeing as individuals and as a community, blacks will be harvested out of existence.

Black Cotton

Malcolm X

"And as soon as the public accepts the fact that the dark-skinned community consists largely of criminals or people who are dirty, then it makes it possible for the power structure to set up a police-state system" (Malcolm X., 1965).

The Overseers

Law enforcement is unfortunately viewed as the modern-day equivalent to the slave overseers of the old South to many low-income black communities. In the old South there were slave codes that established how slaves should be managed, including punishment.

These codes closely resemble the impression many black males have of law enforcement today. Although the legal intent of the police officers' power and style of policing may not be the same as the slave codes, it produces similar results when executed by corrupt officers.

The codes used below are from the Louisiana Slave Codes of 1852, but often one state simply copied the codes and passed them along to another (Rose, 1999).

Slave Code

The slave owes to his master and his family total respect and absolute obedience. He must instantly obey all orders received from them.

Today's parallel

In many poor communities, black males know that if they verbally disrespect, or even talk back to a police officer, the officer may arrest him or worse.

Slave Code

No slave can serve as a witness against a white person.

Today's parallel

There are clear unspoken rules about witnessing anything against law enforcement because of their so-called brotherhood and the potential for backlash in the form of harassment or worse.

Slave Code

Slaves shall always be considered real estate and may be mortgaged according to rules of law.

The Harvesting of Our Youth

Today's parallel

This code speaks to the very point of this book. Black males have become product or property picked from mostly our urban gardens to be sold to private prison corporations, thereby creating a prison economy that also benefits many other industries.

Slave Code

No slave shall be allowed off the plantation without written permission of the master.

Today's parallel

Black males are routinely harassed if they are caught walking or driving through some neighborhoods. I have personally been questioned by police when visiting white friends in their neighborhood. I was asked, "What is your purpose for being in this neighborhood? Let me see your identification." This is racial profiling and harassment by men with guns and can be very humiliating for anyone to endure, but especially a man.

Black Cotton

The Harvesting of Our Youth

Slave Code

If a slave willfully strikes a white person to cause shedding of blood, the slave shall be punished with death.

Today's parallel

It is understood that if a black male even acts like he may strike an officer or reaches in his pocket for a cell phone, he may be shot dead. If he actually strikes an officer, even in self-defense, his life is in jeopardy from that officer and the officer's brotherhood.

These perceptions may not be the norm for most, but when the people that we pay to protect us instead abuse their authority, mistrust and fear spreads like wildfire. We have to weed out bad cops and provide real community accountability for those entrusted to protect us from harm and danger.

In many white communities around America we have perceptions that were born from ignorance and fear. For instance, "If you see a group of young black males walking through the neighborhood, call the police." Another concern that rears its ugly head all too often is that you have to follow blacks when they come into your place of business, because they may steal. These stereotypes often bring forward deeply rooted feelings of prejudice that already exist in the hearts and minds of people. The ignorance has been passed on from generation to generation in many cases, but the fear is often ignited by the politicians using fear to increase the prison population and please the prison lobby.

Those who are paid to serve and protect all Americans have consciously or unconsciously become pawns in a political game. They have become the wage slaves that pick black cotton for the "Prison Masters." These new plantation masters treat urban and rural poor communities like their private plantations. Sadly, as in the days of slavery, many of these overseers are black, and many of the prison guards are black as well. Many of these men and women have completely bought into the mass incarceration of their own people. Others who work for the system know that it is severely broken, but they are forced to support their oppressors because they need to feed their families.

Conservative politicians are the ones often calling for stricter laws. I worked for a private prison firm based in Texas that actively campaigned for very conservative politicians. The firm had no problem asking the employees to make donations to these politicians, stating that it was in our best interest, because the politicians supported the company's agenda. Major companies such as Cornell Companies, Wackenhut Corrections Corporation, and Corrections Corporation of America employ sophisticated lobbyists to protect and expand their market share (Merritt, 2004).

With more than two million people working in law enforcement, it has become one of the largest sectors of the U.S. economy, employing more people than the combined workforces of General Motors, Ford, and Wal-Mart, the three biggest corporate employers in the country (National Commission on Institutions and Alternatives, 2007).

The "get tough on crime" movement, largest sparked by former president Bill Clinton, refers to a set of policies that emphasize punishment as a primary, and often sole, response to crime. Mandatory sentencing, Three strikes, truth-in-sentencing, quality of life policing, zero tolerance, and various other proposals that result in longer and harsher penalties and the elimination of rehabilitation and other programs are all contemporary examples of "tough on crime" policies (Shah, 2005).

The effects of these policies are alarming. Local, state and federal governments have all adopted and implemented these policies resulting in enormous increases in drug arrests, more punitive sentencing

Black Cotton

The Harvesting of Our Youth

proposals, resurgence of the death penalty, and departure from juvenile justice systems, and increased racial profiling and community surveillance. While proponents claim these policies are race-neutral, poor people and people of color are overwhelmingly affected and ensnared by the criminal justice system (Shah, 2005).

I truly believe that the president was sincere in his desire to see crime reduced in our nation; however, I am also sure that he knew that our criminal justice system disproportionately targets those most vulnerable among us. This call to get tough on crime essentially translated into uninhibited permission from the Commander-in-Chief of the United States to go out into our urban and rural gardens and pick black cotton. What a triumph for the prison lobby!

The least resistant and most manageable crop for the overseers and wage slaves is found in poor communities of color. In these communities there is a void of social, economic, and political power. This power is often required to avoid becoming victims of this sick system. High crime rates are one of the unfortunate realities in many poor communities.

Substandard schools, corporate divestment, a lack of adequate financial resources, and many other challenges

Black Cotton

The Harvesting of Our Youth

---

give rise to antisocial behavior. I am not making an excuse for those who willfully break the law, but it becomes more like a fixed fight for many poor people in these communities. On the one hand, America dangles her elusive dream in the faces of the poor daily, but then creates almost insurmountable barriers for certain communities to achieve that dream. The results are higher crime rates and broken homes. Despite this glaring injustice, our so-called leaders ignore the root causes for these conditions while they stand in the public squares of our nation shouting the battle cry, "Get Tough on Crime!"

Look behind the words for a moment. The thin excuses for these calls for crime reduction in our cities and towns don't address the real causes of crime. When we seriously explore the nature of this unsustainable policy of not addressing the root causes for these conditions, we move beyond political pretense and expose the real evil that fuels this system.

It boils down to the love of money or good old-fashioned greed. Billons are generated annually from profits of private prisons, salaries of government agencies, and the residual benefits to other industries from the mass incarceration of the poor.

Black Cotton

The Harvesting of Our Youth

Prison corporations and related industries, politicians that serve the interest of these corporations and law enforcement including the courts, represent an unholy trinity that stands at the helm of the prison industrial complex.

Police officers have a tough job, and I certainly don't want to devalue the work of honest cops. They face many challenges that are unsafe and even life threatening. This being said, we still have to face the fact that there are many downright racist cops and racist policies both written and unwritten that go unchecked.

We have seen many taped incidents of police officers beating young black men and women. If this is not enough we have also seen on tape police officers beating children. Okay, if this is not enough to get you outraged, we know that there have been countless killings of black males from our inner cities by cops who claim they thought their life was threatened, only to find out that the person had no weapon at all. We have seen young black males shot by police officers multiple times, often in the back, while trying to flee.

We must ask ourselves this: If we know about these well-documented cases of police brutality, what about the ones we don't know about?

Black Cotton

The Harvesting of Our Youth

How many young black men are sitting in jails this very hour because of a racist cop or judge?

Here is an even scarier question: How many of these cops are just simple-minded racist pawns being played by the system, and how many are not so simple and actually own stock in the publicly traded prison corporations?

Our law-enforcement officers must be held to the highest moral and ethical standards. We can no longer turn our heads from the injustice that seems woven into the culture of our nation by law enforcement.

How can communities have confidence in law enforcement, when time and time again police officers make it clear that they are not serving and protecting the community, but in many cases are predators themselves?

Another insidious aspect of the law enforcement culture is the silent nod of support given by leadership to street-level officers who abuse their authority when policing poor communities. This is like the so-called "No Torture Policy" of our military, while justifying the continued use of water boarding. Some would have us believe that things aren't that bad, but time and time again we see police officers abusing their authority and judges throwing away the key. Black and brown people from poor communities around our country need not be convinced of these realties, they see it daily.

Let's review the facts:

Fact: African-Americans comprise nearly two-thirds of all drug offenders admitted to state prison, though they constitute only 13% of American drug users. According to a recent Human Rights Watch report, black men are admitted to state prison on drug charges at a rate that is 13.4 times greater than that of white men - with rates up to 57 times greater in some states. In Maryland and Illinois, blacks constitute 90% of all people sent to prison for drug law violations (Human Rights Watch, 2000).

Fact: Possession of five grams of crack cocaine mandated the same minimum sentence as 500 grams of powder cocaine. Whites are more likely to have powder and blacks are more likely to have crack (Henderson, 2009).

Fact: Almost 1.4 million African American males, or 14% of the adult black male population, are currently disenfranchised as a result of felony convictions. Black men represent more than 36% of the total disenfranchised male population in the U.S., although they make up less than 15% of American males (Drug Policy Alliance, 2002).

Fact: Communities of color are disproportionately affected by increasingly militarized local law enforcement. Nearly 90% of police departments have a paramilitary unit, whose most common use is serving drug-related search warrants - generally "no-knock" entries into private residences, which defy the Fourth Amendment prohibition of "unreasonable searches and seizures" (Drug Policy Alliance, 2002).

Fact: Regardless of similar or equal levels of illicit drug use during pregnancy, black women are 10 times more likely than white women to be reported to child welfare agencies for prenatal drug use (Drug Policy Alliance, 2002).

Anyone who looks at the current situation with a sober mind must surmise that our current system is critically flawed and racially biased.

Black Cotton

Rev. Jesse L. Jackson

"That which goes on in the frat houses falls within the limits of 'youthful indiscretion', but when it happens on the street corner, they call it 'target practice" (Jackson, 2000).

Black Cotton

The Harvesting of Our Youth

Fact

Nationwide, one in every 20 black men over the age of 18 is in prison. In five states, between one in 13 and one in 14 black men is in prison. This compares to one in 180 white men (Human Rights Watch, 2000).

3lack Cotton

The Harvesting of Our Youth

The Harvest

During slavery times the children slaves used to sing a song about the time to harvest the cotton:

"First day white, next day red, third day from my birth, I'm dead."

This song tells the tale about what happens to the cotton plant upon reaching a certain stage of maturity. After about eleven weeks, the flowers on the cotton plant begin to wither and fall off. The process takes about three days; hence the song. In about seven more weeks, the plant matures, and after seven to ten weeks, the cotton is ready for harvesting (Scherer, 1916).

When is black cotton harvested? Instead of measuring the maturity period in weeks, the prison corporations measure black cotton maturity in years. Black males in

---

Black Cotton

The Harvesting of Our Youth

America begin to lose their innocence during their preteen years and are exposed to all sorts of social challenges growing up in poor communities. Like the cotton plant, their flowers of innocence begin to wither at about age eleven. Planted firmly in the fertile soil of the American ghetto, whether urban or rural, many young blacks adopt antisocial behavior to survive the unfair social conditions they experience day to day. These children watch their fathers and other role models carted off to prison and jails regularly. They see the type violence, that if witnessed by white suburban children, the community would fly in plane loads of psychologists to counsel them. Young blacks watch television and see the extreme wealth of others, and wonder if they will ever have any real success. They also see our government, whose flag they pledge allegiance too, spend billions to liberate people around the world. Intern black youth get little to no genuine concern for their wellbeing Similar to the cotton plant, if these youths survive the initial weeds and disease in their communities they become ripe for harvesting in about seven more years at age eighteen.

Fact: Fifty percent of black males between the ages of eighteen and thirty-five are involved with the criminal justice system (Stewart, 2002).

$\mathcal{B}$lack Cotton

The Harvesting of Our Youth

Let's take a closer look at the fertilization of black cotton.

Proliferation of crack cocaine

The proliferation of crack cocaine has been one of the greatest contributors to the mass incarceration of young black males in America. During the 1980s the drug hit the street like a roaring lion seeking to devour all in its path. A cheaper form of its parent drug, powder cocaine, crack is highly addictive. Crack provides the user with a temporary sense of euphoria that lasts only a few minutes. After the initial high, the user needs to get the next "hit" by any means possible. Those who use crack for long periods do so much damage to their brains that they become almost subhuman. They roam the streets for days at a time and often steal, sell their bodies, and sink to pitiful and incomprehensible moral lows. The demoralization takes on other forms for the crack addict.

They become emaciated, unemployable, antisocial, and downright undesirable people to be around. Their families and friends are also damaged from their countless efforts to save the addict, including drug treatment and mental asylum commitments. The addict leaves the treatment center and/or the mental hospital with the strong conviction to remain drug free, and

Black Cotton

The Harvesting of Our Youth

many do for days, weeks, and even months only to begin the vicious cycle again. The community refers to the crack addict as a "crack head" or "hype". These labels detach the community in some way from the person who has become addicted and segregates the addict in a dark subculture where he or she becomes a new resident. The problem with this kind of segregation is that the addicts are still members of the community. They are fathers, mothers, sons and daughters of families that have been damaged by the demon drug.

If no solution is found, the addict continues to use the drug until permanent removal from society occurs. This removal can happen in three ways: jails, institutions, or death. Crack truly created the perfect storm for the prison system. Countless numbers of young black males have fallen to this vicious attack on their communities. I call it an attack because the proliferation of crack was no accident. We now know that the United States government played a significant role in beginning this epidemic.

According to an investigative report by Garry Webb, published by the San *Jose Mercury News*, there was a link between the CIA and the crack trade in America. There have been many articles written both supporting and refuting the connection. Critics claim that Webb's report was sloppy and unsubstantiated.

*B*lack Cotton

The Harvesting of Our Youth

The Dark Alliance

Webb investigated Nicaraguans linked to the CIA-backed Contras who had allegedly smuggled cocaine into the U.S. which was then distributed as crack cocaine into Los Angeles and funneled profits to the Contras. Webb also alleged that this influx of Nicaraguan supplied cocaine sparked and significantly fueled the widespread crack epidemic that swept through urban areas. According to Webb, the CIA was aware of the cocaine transactions and the large shipments of drugs into the U.S. by the Contra personnel and directly aided drug dealers to raise money for the Contras (Feder, 2005).

Webb's reporting generated a controversy, and his paper backed away from the story, this effectively ended Webb's career as a mainstream media figure. In 2004, Webb was found dead from two gunshot wounds to the head, which the coroner's office later judged as a suicide.

There was a government investigation headed by one time Democratic presidential nominee Senator John Kerry that exposed some interesting facts.

Kerry's Report

The Kerry Committee report was based on hearings chaired by Senator John Kerry and found the United States Department of State had paid drug traffickers. Some of these payments were after the traffickers had been indicted by federal law enforcement agencies on drug charges or while traffickers were under active investigation by these same agencies. The Kerry investigation lasted two and a half years and heard scores of witnesses; its report was released on April 13, 1989. The final report was 400 pages, with an additional 600-page appendix. The committee stated, "It is clear that individuals who provided support for the Contras were involved in drug trafficking...and elements of the Contras themselves knowingly received financial and material assistance from drug traffickers"(Engelberg, 1986).

Other investigations revealed that the CIA knowingly turned a blind eye to drugs actually being shipped on planes contracted by the U.S. government.

The government involvement in drug trafficking may come as shock to some, but to the poor communities negatively impacted by the drug trade, it probably is not such a shock. We see our young men being snatched off the streets and sent to prison for years for a situation that our own government helped to create.

Bringing the issues of government involvement in the drug trade closer to home are the corrupt law enforcement officers who are engaged in the drug game themselves. I have personally spoken with officers who say they know of cops selling drugs in inner-city communities. This is no secret in poor communities. Just drive through any neighborhood that has a lot of crime and drugs, and you will see that everyone knows where the drug houses are, but the police drive right by. This arrangement creates a frustrating situation because on the one hand drugs are killing our communities, and on the other we don't want our young men who have been caught up in a government-backed attack on our communities to go to jail for years.

This situation creates an atmosphere of mistrust between law enforcement and the communities they serve. It also creates mistrust among residents in these communities, because they really want to have better and safer living conditions, but the systems represent a fixed fight.

Black Cotton

The Harvesting of Our Youth

Pervasive Poverty

Hurricane Katrina blew the cover off the bed of American inner-city poverty. The storm rolled in like a voice from heaven, saying, "See what you have allowed to exist amid such great wealth and prosperity?" The voice not only shouted this message to government and corporations, but to the church, which seemed to be concerned only about their temples and overseas missions.

Why has the voice of the shepherd gone unheard by those who claimed to be his sheep? What has happened to our fighters for social and economic justice in the church? Have posh lifestyles and fear of economic insecurity silenced our warriors for justice? Or have we simply given up?

We see many of our churches fighting for market share, in the form of memberships, and can't see that they need to combine their resources in order to fight for the poor.

As with many other social ills, the vast majority of those experiencing hunger in America are black. Those that claim to hear the voice of God must get past their differences with each other and begin hearing the voices of hungry children, if we are to have progress in poor communities

Black Cotton

The Harvesting of Our Youth

The fact is, extreme poverty still exists in America, and it fuels crime and fills prison beds. Contributing to the high incarceration rates among black males is lack of living wage jobs in inner-city communities. Many inner-city communities seem to be trapped in a perpetual state of lack and hopelessness. I often thought one of the reasons many black males are willing to risk incarceration and even death for selling drugs is that they think their communities are prisoners to poverty anyway. Hungry children and lack of hope can turn the best of us into criminals.

My mother worked hard to raise my sister and me. She often worked multiple low-paying jobs to feed our family. I saw her cry over lack of support from my absentee father who was strung out on crack cocaine. A woman of courage and faith, she never gave up and worked whenever and wherever she could to make ends meet. Other family members chipped in to help, whether it was cash or simply sharing food. I recall long waits at the public aid office where she received food stamps to buy food. When the food stamps came, it was like Christmas, because I got to go grocery shopping with her and pick out items I liked. She always made it fun and kept us from feeling her real frustration.

Black Cotton

The Harvesting of Our Youth

As I grew older and really needed a father to help me find my way as a teenager, my father simply was not available. I became increasingly aware of our financial situation and began thinking of ways to make money. I became a very frustrated, off-balance teenager with no real male role models. I was a perfect target for the crack epidemic and I eventually fell to the streets. As a result, my mother had two people she loved who were lost to the beast that was ravaging our community. She never gave up on me and I survived and lived to help others survive as well.

The sad fact is that there are many mothers who don't see their loved ones come back from the brink of death and many people still surviving on limited government assistance and below-living-wage jobs. Unfortunately, many family homes have become revolving doors for the prison system because of deeply rooted poverty.

According to a report on poverty, written by Rachel Bogardus Drew, "Residents of high poverty areas often earn incomes so low that they cannot afford even the rents and housing costs on the dilapidated units in their neighborhoods. In 2000, almost a third of households in these areas still paid at least half their income for housing, in spite of living in some of the worst housing conditions" (Rachel Bogardus Drew, 2006).

$\mathcal{B}$lack Cotton

Poverty is a key ingredient in preparing the harvest for the prison system. If we do not eliminate extreme poverty in our nation, people will do whatever they can to survive.

Poor Education

The abysmal failure of inner-city schools is well documented. The cost of this failure is felt primarily by urban families, but it has more far-reaching effects on society as a whole. Our poorest kids are trapped in communities where even many of the teachers have lost all hope for better educational outcomes. The sad fact is that poor kids do poorly.

A Brookings policy brief titled "A New Era in Urban Education?" states, "Urban schools enroll 24% of all public school students in the United States, 35% of poor students, and 43% of minority students. In a massive survey of urban education, *Education Week* concluded that "most fourth graders who live in U.S. cities can't read and understand a simple children's book, and most eighth graders can't use arithmetic to solve a practical problem." Slightly more than half of big-city students are unable to graduate from high school in the customary four years, and many of those who do

Black Cotton

The Harvesting of Our Youth

---

manage to graduate are ill-prepared for higher education or the workplace" (Ravitch, 1998).

An article on *Urbanite*, a Baltimore urban information Web site by R. Darryl Foxworth he reports, "The deepening plight of black men has finally—if only briefly—been recognized by the press and academicians. Several disturbing trends have been uncovered by recent studies and news reports: 72% of black male high school dropouts in their twenties are jobless; more than half of all black men residing in inner cities fail to complete high school; 60% of black male high-school dropouts have served jail time by their mid-thirties; 50% of black men in their twenties lacking a college education are jobless; only 25% of black males ages 18 to 24 attend college; and black male high-school dropouts in their late twenties are more likely to be behind bars (34%) than working (30%). Sadly, such frightening statistics fail to surprise me, and in Baltimore—a city mired in violence, drugs, and failing schools—the black male high-school dropout rate has been as high as 76% in recent years, well above the national average of 50% for inner-city black males" (Foxworth, 2007).

Unfortunately, the trends reported by Foxworth are status quo in inner-city minority communities nationally. Education is critical to social and economic growth in this country. We know what it takes to make a successful school, but many of the most talented educators and financial resources are found only in suburbia and private schools. My son Malcolm, now eight years old, has always gone to the very best school that I could afford. I often watched in amazement at the difference in the quality of education and level of student performance he received versus children his same age in the public school system. He now attends a public school in a nice community, and the quality of the education rivals that of the Christian private school he once attended. He is currently in third grade. His reading and math scores are on a fifth-grade level.

I realize that there are many contributing factors to Malcolm's progress in school, including educated parents who take time with him, exposure to many other cultures in a diverse learning environment, and great teachers who see his parents often. These factors don't exist in every home, and it is unrealistic to expect them to; however, we must leave no stone unturned if we are going to save our kids from the prison vultures.

Given the critical condition of our school system, such as a 76% dropout rate among black males in the city of Baltimore, you would expect there to be a national outcry. If a private or public school in a wealthy community had the same dropout rates, you would hear

The Harvesting of Our Youth

such a public outcry that it would shake the very foundation of the White House. Teachers would be fired and counselors and psychologists would be flown in from around the country.

So I ask you, what is it about poor black youth that makes our political leaders and church leaders so silent? What is it about our black children that keep CNN, ABC, CBS, FOX, and TBN from treating it as a national crisis? What is it about our black children that keep some black entertainers from financing private schools and foundations to confront the educational and poverty issues? But then again, maybe it's not their problem; besides, they are just entertainers, right? I guess kids in these inner-city communities should simply continue longing to be like the pro-ball player and buy his gym shoes, if they can afford a pair.

The reality is that we will need the collective efforts of the black wealth in America if we are going to see real change in our public schools and poor communities. I know many of our entertainer have charitable foundations, but we need them to do more and take an active and genuine role in making change happen.

We will likely lose thousands of our youth to prison corporations and their henchmen that profit from a failed public school system. What we are really fighting is the evil behind the system, or those that pull the purse strings of the prison industrial complex.

Black Cotton

The Harvesting of Our Youth

Dr. Michael Eric Dyson

"There is a vicious prison system that hungers for young black and brown bodies. The more young black and brown folk are thrown in jail, the more cells are built, and the more money made. It has been well documented that we spend far more money on penitentiaries than university education for poor black and brown males" (Dyson, 2009).

The Cotton Gin

Eli Whitney was the inventor of the cotton gin and a pioneer in the mass production of cotton. Whitney was born in Westboro, Massachusetts, on December 8, 1765, and died on January 8, 1825. He graduated from Yale College in 1792. By April 1793, Whitney had designed and constructed the cotton gin, a machine that automated the separation of cottonseed from the short-staple cotton fiber (National Inventors Hall of Fame Foundation, Inc, 2002).

I submit to you that the prison system is the modern-day equivalent of the cotton gin for black males. As slaves we used to pick cotton in this country, and now, through the development of a profitable prison system, we have become the cotton. Black males represent 50% of the 2,000,000 inmates currently incarcerated in our nation.

Black Cotton

The Harvesting of Our Youth

This is a staggering figure, because blacks make up only about 13% of the population in America.

The gin was designed to separate the cotton from its seed so it could be sold on the mass market. Similarly, black males are being separated from their seed, their children, to be sold for profit to private prisons. Inmates create jobs for hundreds of thousands of law-enforcement employees as well as employees in related industries. Industries that profit from mass incarceration include the hotels that house family members who visit prisoners, contractors that sell all types of products to prisons, prison guards and counselors, high-paid wardens, and construction companies that get high-paying contracts to construct new prisons.

As if all this profiting from crime were not enough, there is political gain from incarceration as well. According to a New York Prison initiative, Prisoners of The Census, "The Census Bureau counts people in prison as if they were residents of the communities where they are incarcerated, even though they remain legal residents of the places they lived prior to incarceration. As Census data is used to apportion political power at all levels of government, crediting thousands of disproportionately urban and minority men to other communities has staggering implications for modern American democracy" (Lotke, 2004).

Black Cotton

The Harvesting of Our Youth

The situation in New York is also a problem nationally. Again it gives further credence to my assertion in the introduction of this book that the prison system supports a culture of kidnapping. We see thousands upon thousands of young black males being swept off the streets of urban communities and sold too many private prisons that house them in communities that count them as residents, which shifts political power from the poor.

It is clear to see why the system does not want inmates to vote. The conditions inside many of these human-spirit grinders called prisons are abominable. Prison beatings by guards and other inmates are a regular occurrence; so are rapes. Drug trafficking on the part of prison employees is also normal and expected. We see many injuries and deaths annually within the walls of confinement. Somehow, many prison guards and officials feel like it's their duty to punish inmates once they come to prison. This attitude is twisted, not to mention unlawful, but it's the so-called law that got us into this situation in the first place.

Prisoners are sentenced to confinement as punishment for their crimes; they are not to be punished while confined. The taking away of their freedom is the punishment, and while confined they should be

---

*B*lack Cotton

protected and treated with dignity and respect at all times.

As with law enforcement, the prison system creates an "us against them" culture that often turns violent and harmful to inmates. Gangs run many prison yards and are allowed to conduct illegal activities in prisons. Rehabilitation is almost nonexistent.

I once worked for the Mississippi Department of Corrections as a counselor and was informed during my official job orientation that the Mississippi Department of Correction does not claim to rehabilitate anyone and is simply protecting the public from criminals. The problem with this notion of not rehabilitating offenders is that most will eventually return to their communities, and without adequate education and life skills, they will likely offend again. The prison system creates the revolving-door syndrome known as recidivism.

In addition to the obvious injustice in the human cotton gin, prisoners work for little or no wages to produce furniture, clothing, and other products as well as provide labor and construction services that will never benefit them or their families, but rather further entrench those who maintain this corruption.

$\mathcal{B}$lack Cotton

The Harvesting of Our Youth

Mother Jones magazine conducted an exhaustive analysis of the incarceration rates in the USA and its statistics taken from various federal and international sources. The analysis shows a frightening picture of this nation as a locked-down nation for a large segment of the population.

Black Cotton

The Harvesting of Our Youth

According to *Mother Jones*, the states that have the largest Black prison populations are these:

State	Black Population	Black Prison Population
Georgia	29%	64%
Ohio	12%	52%
Iowa	2%	24%
Minnesota	3%	37%
Wisconsin	6%	48%
Illinois	15%	65%
Missouri	11%	45%
Arkansas	16%	52%
Louisiana	33%	76%
Mississippi	36%	75%
Alabama	26%	65%
Tennessee	16%	53%

Black Cotton

The Harvesting of Our Youth

Kentucky	7%	36%
Indiana	8%	42%
Michigan	14%	55%
South Carolina	30%	69%
North Carolina	22%	64%
Virginia	20%	68%
Pennsylvania	10%	56%
New York	15%	51%
Delaware	19%	63%
Maryland	28%	77%
Connecticut	9%	47%
New Jersey	13%	64%
Rhode Island	4%	30%

Black Cotton

The Harvesting of Our Youth

The report goes on to state, "The states where blacks are not being placed in prison as a matter of course are Hawaii, Maine, New Hampshire, and Idaho, even though their general populations are small. Most of the states with a majority of black prisoners are found in the South; however, Maryland, which isn't generally viewed as a Southern state, has the largest percentage of Black prisoners—77%. But Wisconsin, with a tiny black population of 6%, has a black prison population of 48%, and Mississippi, with the largest black population of 36%, has a black prison population of 75%" (Mother Jones magazine , 2001).

Attorney Barbara Ratliff, an L.A.-based reparations activist, said the prison industrial complex's extension of the slave plantation plays out in a pattern of behavior that black people must study, to survive. "I'm not talking about behavior of the individual incarcerate, but the pattern of treatment that digs into institutional racism. Corporate profit from prisons is no different than how slave owners received benefits from their labor, and that impact remained even after slavery. For instance, freed blacks were arrested and put on chain gangs for their labor, which continued to benefit slave owners, so this is no accident," she said.

Given the staggering disparity of race and class in the rates of incarceration, any reasonable person would have

Black Cotton

to conclude that the system is launching an all-out war against black males nationwide. This war is a silent and deadly one that seems to be completely ignored by our mainstream media, political officials, and church leaders.

The new cash crop of young black men seems to be endless. As long as those who administer the system hold on to old biases and preconceived notions about black intelligence and inferiority, the real evil behind this system will go unchecked in their demonic disregard for human rights.

Black Cotton

The Harvesting of Our Youth

Tupac Amaru Shakur

"Lookin' through my high school yearbook - Reminiscin' of the tears as the years took - One homie, two homie, three homies - POOF -We used to have troops but now there's no more youth to shoot — God come save the misbegotten -Lost ghetto souls of **Black Cotton**" (Shakur, 2004)

The Seed

The movie *Left Behind* tells the story of Christians who have missed the opportunity to go with God when he returns for his people. This is known as "The Rapture." In the movie people all over the world disappear mysteriously in the last days, and the world is terrified. Many Christians realize what has taken place and know they have been left behind to suffer the "Great Tribulation" (Sarin, 2000).

The feeling of being left behind is experienced by children of incarcerated parents daily. These kids have their world turned upside down and face hardship and suffering because their parents have been harvested by a corrupt criminal justice system. Many of these kids were already struggling below the poverty line in single-parent homes. Once their parents go to jail they suffer even more, often being placed with grandparents or distant relatives for care, many of whom live in poverty themselves. These kids often end up in the Foster Care system or worse, such as becoming homeless.

The children who are fortunate enough to have a decent place to live and have nurturing environments have a better chance of becoming healthy adults. They also face serious emotional problems that often carry over into their personal relationships, education, and outlook on life. These children consequently have a great likelihood of falling on the same fertile ground of our poor communities that produce the future crops of black cotton. Below is a chart showing the intergenerational behaviors as they relate to crime and incarceration. Children of incarcerated parents are more likely to follow in their parent's footsteps.

Intergenerational Behaviors, Crime, and Incarceration

Childhood Trauma	Emotional Response	Reactive Behavior	Coping Pattern	Criminal Activity
Physical abuse	Anger	Physical aggression	Fighting with peers	Assault
Parent-child separation	Sadness, grief	Withdrawal	Substance abuse	Drug possession
Witness to violence	Anxiety	Hyper vigilance	Gang activity	Accessory to homicide
Parental substance abuse	Anger	Verbal aggression	Asocial behavior (lying, stealing)	Fraud
Sexual molestation	Fear, anxiety	Sexualized behavior	Promiscuity	Prostitution

Chart Source: Dr. Denise Johnston, "Effects of Parental Incarceration," in Gabel and Johnston, p. 81.

Black Cotton

The Harvesting of Our Youth

The fertile ground of many poor inner-city communities rivals that of many war zones in the world. For instance, I was working as an addiction counselor in a Chicago neighborhood, where my office was on the fourth floor. I could see clearly down to street level, and I watched as children walk home from school. A gun battle between rival gangs broke out on the corner, a common occurrence in that particular community. It was sad to see young men trying to kill each other. But even more heartbreaking, were the responses of the kids walking home; they simply kept walking. That's right, they didn't duck, run, or hide, for they had been conditioned to live in violence.

While working as a counselor, I often saw veterans who suffered from post-traumatic stress disorder, PTSD. PTSD is an anxiety disorder that can develop after exposure to one or more terrifying events that threatened to cause or caused grave physical harm. It is a severe and ongoing emotional reaction to an extreme psychological trauma. This stressor may involve someone's actual death, a threat to the patient's or someone else's life, serious physical injury, or threat to physical or psychological integrity. The threat overwhelms the person's usual psychological coping defenses. In some cases PTSD can be the result of profound psychological and emotional trauma, apart

Black Cotton

The Harvesting of Our Youth

---

from any actual physical harm. Often, however, physical and psychological traumas are combined to cause PTSD. PTSD is a condition distinct from traumatic stress, which has less intensity and duration, and combat stress reaction, which is transitory. PTSD has also been recognized in the past as railway spine, shellshock, traumatic war neurosis, or post-traumatic stress syndrome (National Center for PTSD , 2008).

People suffer from this disorder because they have seen so much violence that it affects their ability to function. They often attempt to cope with the extreme stress by using and/or abusing drugs and alcohol. It is clear that our young people have experienced many traumatic situations, some far more than others, but who is concerned about getting the help they need? Our government spends many billions of dollars to fight for the liberation of other nations, and yet it ignores the needs of the inner-city poor children. Politicians are clear about the severity of this issue and yet do nothing substantive to address it. They are clear about who is being affected and what it represents for the people in power in this nation. They allow it because it produces product for the largest criminal justice system in the world.

Black Cotton

The Harvesting of Our Youth

While our most precious commodity, our children, are being attacked, where is our voice of justice and faith? Why are we not willing to shout, march, preach, fight, and die for the safety and wellbeing of our babies?

We can no longer afford to support so-called leaders if they are not fighting to change this sick system. If they are not willing to put themselves in harm's way for our kids, then they can't protect them.

Black Cotton

Dr. Angela Davis

"In 1966, when the Black Panther Party was founded, they used guns and law books symbolically. The call was not for people to use arms against the police, but to stand up against police brutality and to stand up to police violation of rights of the community" (Davis, 1998).

Black Cotton

The Harvesting of Our Youth

Fact

"Most drug offenders are white. Five times as many whites use drugs as blacks. Yet blacks comprise the great majority of drug offenders sent to prison. The solution to this racial inequity is not to incarcerate more whites, but to reduce the use of prison for low-level drug offenders and to increase the availability of substance abuse treatment"(Human Rights Watch, 2000).

The Black Cotton Agenda

In this chapter I will offer suggestions as to how we as nation should confront the challenge of dismantling the prison industrial complex, or at the very least reduce its effect on poor communities. I provide a nine-point agenda that does not present new ideas but encourages the expansion of evidenced base practices that have had some success in various communities around the country.

I hope that you see how you as an individual, neighborhood, church, nonprofit organization, school, law enforcement agency, political leader, or ex-offender can see how to undertake all or part of this agenda and begin to make a difference in your community.

Black Cotton

The Harvesting of Our Youth

The Agenda

1. Release of all nonviolent offenders who have been locked up for drug-related crimes

The disproportionate incarceration rate of black and brown males for nonviolent drug offenses is well documented. There has been an overwhelming outcry from the public that has fallen on deaf ears in Washington. Just as with the slave revolts of history, oppressed people will eventually rise up against their oppressors.

In minority communities, resistance to oppression often begins with our religious leaders in response to the outcry of their communities. One such response was made in an appeal to the Clinton Administration by the Criminal Justice Policy Foundation. The Foundation headed an initiative called the Coalition for Jubilee Clemency, which organized a state-by-state coalition of religious leaders to make an appeal to President Bill Clinton to grant clemency to, low-level, nonviolent federal drug offenders. The appeal had a certain measure of success, and near the end of his term, President Clinton granted clemency to twenty-three such offenders (The Coalition for Jubilee Clemency, 2002).

Black Cotton

The Harvesting of Our Youth

Although many organizations around the country are fighting for this cause, we are far from national policy reform that would ensure justice for poor individuals and their families. In light of what we know about how crack cocaine was proliferated nationally, we need those who would be true leaders in Washington to call for the release of ALL nonviolent drug offenders on the state and federal levels. These offenders should be mandated to educational programs and provided the opportunity to make at least a living wage. For those who are suffering from the disease of addiction, as opposed to selling drugs, we should mandate them to one year of intensive secured residential treatment. This treatment can be offered in a correctional setting, as long as the primary purpose for the stay is rehabilitation.

2. **Redirect prison funding towards alternatives to incarceration and community based re-entry programs and services.**

It offends reason to continue supporting policies that we know don't work. Time and time again we see individuals and groups challenge the status quo by successfully providing evidence of gains in this area of criminal justice reform; however, the government as a whole seems to be unable or unwilling to pass

---

Black Cotton

---

meaningful legislation to support those heroic efforts. Below is a sample of what everyone in Washington knows about the cost savings of alternatives to incarceration and re-entry programs.

We know what works:

The New York State drug court system saved $254 million in prison-related expenses by diverting 18,000 nonviolent drug offenders into drug courts in lieu of incarceration (City of Chicago, n.d.).
Two recently completed studies in California demonstrate a minimal savings of $18 million a year through the California drug courts. The studies concluded that California's investment of $14 million, in combination with other funds, created a total cost avoidance of $43.3 million over a two-year period. Another study of three adult drug courts in California documented cost avoidance averaging $200,000 annually per court per one hundred participants
A study of six drug courts in Washington State estimates that the average drug court participant produces $6,779 in benefits that stem from the estimated 13% reductions in recidivism. Those benefits are made up of $3,759 in avoided criminal justice system costs paid by taxpayers and $3,020 in avoided costs to victims.

The Harvesting of Our Youth

For every dollar spent on drug court in Dallas, Texas, $9.43 in tax-dollar savings was realized over a forty-month period (Administrative Office of the Courts, 2004).
The funds that will be saved as a result of the release of nonviolent drug offenders will provide funding for the re-entry services and drug courts and other alternatives to incarceration.

3. **Give tax incentives to corporations that create good paying jobs in low-income inner-city communities.**

Instead of investing in the mass incarceration of mostly nonviolent offenders, we need to develop strategies to provide living-wage jobs in poor communities.
State and local governments both created tax- and non-tax incentives for job creation in urban and rural communities; however, many of these projects either don't pay a living wage and/or don't actually create enough jobs to make a difference in severely impoverished communities.
Many companies that pay good salaries often argue that there is not enough skilled labor to get their staffing needs met; therefore they must go outside of poor communities to satisfy their skilled-labor requirements.

*B*lack Cotton

The Harvesting of Our Youth

Many companies, to their credit, offer incentives and training programs to potential employees, but these programs are not practiced enough to make a real impact.

Currently, state and local governments offer the following incentives to companies willing to creative jobs:

Statutory Tax Incentives

Statutory tax incentives include income and franchise tax credits, such as job tax credits, investment tax credits, and research and development tax credits; sales and use tax credits; apportionment factor adjustments and tax-base modifications; and incentives for locating in targeted economic development areas. Statutory incentives are available to any company that engages in qualified activity and meets the applicable requirements (Uminski & Chizek, 2008).

Discretionary Tax Incentives

Discretionary tax incentives are awarded on a case-by-case basis to entice particularly desirable employers to relocate or expand in an area. Examples might include certain state tax credits, enterprise zone benefits, property tax abatements, sales and use tax exemptions, and monies for infrastructure improvements and human resource needs (Uminski & Chizek, 2008).

Non-Tax Incentives

State and local governments also offer a broad range of discretionary non-tax incentives, such as direct grants; low-interest financing and bonds; infrastructure grants; real estate cost reductions; utility-rate reductions; and training subsidies, credits, and grants. For instance, an economic development agency may provide training incentives to companies that create new jobs or invest in a new technology that requires training; or incentives might be granted to support ongoing training necessary to satisfy certain guidelines, like OSHA standards (Uminski & Chizek, 2008).

These programs for job attraction are a good start, but we must do more. If we expect to see real change in poor communities where we have more black men in prison than in college, we must provide the kind of incentives to companies that allow them to develop and implement innovative job creation strategies, while remaining competitive in their particular industries.

4. Provide funding for community-based mental health services.

During my time working as an alcohol and drug counselor in community-based and correctional-based settings, I have witnessed firsthand the mental health crisis we have in America. Because of the overwhelming demand and lack of adequate funding for mental health services, particularly resident treatment, our jails and prisons have become the mental health industry's dumping grounds of our nation. Many people suffering from treatable mental health conditions end up in our prison system or under a bridge because we do not see this problem as a national priority.

Previously in chapter, The Seed, I discussed the effects on the children left behind by incarcerated parents and the fact that many of these youths are exposed to traumatic situations that may affect their mental health. In communities where poverty, gang violence, shootings, beatings, robberies, and police brutality are common amid the media's flaunting of glamour and wealth, we can easily see why youths and adults develop a sense of hopelessness, desperation, and even depression.

We need great mental health counselors in schools, working with children from kindergarten through grade twelve, as well as adequate funding for mental health organizations to set up shop in the poorest communities. In addition, we need to institute programs like mental health courts, largely advocated by Mental Health America. Similar to drug court or jail diversion programs, offenders will be thoroughly evaluated for mental health conditions that require treatment. Offenders will then be mandated to receive community-based help, as opposed to incarceration, where it is virtually impossible to provide high-quality mental health treatment.

5. **Restore the full personal credit history for people affected by the drug trade and systemic poverty.**

One of the most unfair setups in poor communities affected by the drug epidemic and other extreme social and economic conditions is the so-called secret formula that consumer-reporting agencies, also known as credit bureaus, use to calculate credit scores. These formulas have been studied by various researchers that have made a clear argument about the unfairness to the poor in the credit-scoring models. Access to credit is critical for wealth building in America, and many poor people who pay their bills and struggle to survive can't ever get

---

ahead. Many people unaffected by extreme poverty typically argue that the poor need more financial management counseling and education. Much of this argument is true. We should all keep our money management skills up to par; however, there is a deeper and more sinister problem with the credit-reporting agencies. They have formulas for calculating our credit scores based on a formula that we as Americas are fully accountable to, but have no access to. The other problem is that studies have shown that the formulas do not account for situational factors that contribute to financial distress.

According to a study commissioned by the Bank for International Settlements:

"For example, by not including individual situational circumstances, the model would implicitly treat someone who performs poorly while experiencing a temporary health problem the same as someone with similar performance while healthy. Similarly, by not controlling for local economic factors, a credit history scoring model would assign the same risk level to a person who performs poorly during a temporary period of adverse local economic conditions."

The Harvesting of Our Youth

Just as with many other challenges we face in poor communities, our leaders know these things, but for some reason they are unable or simply unwilling to do anything meaningful to change them. Also, it is not simply enough to change it going forward, but we must clean up the mess left behind that will affect generations to come.

6. **Fund community-based alternative education centers that offer evidence-based tutoring programs for youth and adults seeking to complete high school**

The overall American dropout rate is sad, to say the least, but the black male dropout rate, especially in poor communities, has reached epidemic levels. We can no longer tolerate a child of any socioeconomic background dropping out of school. To sit idly and watch youth after youth, make the decision, for whatever reason to quit school is the real crime and we as adults are responsible for changing this sad situation.

A high-quality education is one of the keys to freedom from poverty and to closing the door of recidivism in our criminal justice system. There are many evidence-based alternative education models that are working in communities across our nation, but there needs to be a

Black Cotton

federal commitment to implement a program nationally. Preventing the next generation from dropping out has to be paramount on our list of priorities, but we must also recapture those who have already fallen through the cracks of our broken educational system.

7. **Restructure law enforcement leadership and officials that are hired by the communities they serve.**

The gang style policing of poor communities must end. I know that not all law enforcement officials are involved in predatory behavior, but the fact is, if you are silent about these issues and don't lift a hand to change them, then you are part of the problem. To most people in poor communities, our law enforcement groups have begun to resemble some kind of secret society. This fact, along with common police beatings of suspects, unjustified murders of typically black males, and racial profiling, has caused a sense of fear and an "us-against-them" attitude in poor communities.

My proposed solution is simple; make all people in enforcement leadership accountable to the communities they serve, district by district, ward by ward, and neighborhood by neighborhood, if necessary. Full accountability through the election process will go a long way to ensure that communities get rid of bad cops and citizens feel like the people they pay to protect and serve them are actually doing so.

8. **Offer high school and college education in every prison in America.**

For some reason many people believe that people go to jail to be punished, and therefore inmates don't deserve anything other than hard time. This could not be further from the truth. When people are sentenced to jail, they are given their punishment at that time, and that time only. The only punishment is the taking of their freedom, period. They don't go to jail or prison to be abused in any way. This is torture, not justice. We can no longer act as if these American citizens won't return to society one day, because the vast majority of them will. It stands to reason that we as citizens truly concerned about the betterment of our country would do all we could to ensure full rehabilitation of inmates. We need to see all inmates as future returning citizens who need help, not more punishment, once they get to jail. Access to a good education while incarcerated may be more than many were given in their communities. If we are going to assist with changing lives for the better, reducing the recidivism rate, thereby ensuring the public safety, we must provide high school and college educational opportunities inside our nation's prisons.

9. Restore rights to all ex-offenders in America.

Jeff Manza, Ph.D., professor of sociology and political science and associate director and faculty fellow at the Institute for Policy Research at Northwestern University, and Christopher Uggen, Ph.D., distinguished McKnight professor of sociology at the University of Minnesota, stated in their 2006 book *Locked Out: Felon Disenfranchisement and American Democracy*: "Ex-offenders face legal restrictions on employment, they lack access to public social benefits and public housing, they are ineligible for many educational benefits, and they may have lost parental rights. In many states, their criminal history is a matter of public record, readily searchable for anyone who wants to know. Research on the lives of ex-offenders has consistently demonstrated they have difficulty finding jobs and a safe place to live, reconnecting with their friends and families, and making their way in a world where they are branded, often for life, by the stigma of a criminal conviction" (Manza & Uggen, 2006).

Black Cotton

The Harvesting of Our Youth

These legal and social barriers make it very difficult to stay on the straight and narrow path. If ex-offenders return from paying their debts to society, then that society should want to see them become healthy, productive, and taxpaying citizens. Many people believe once a convict, always a convict. This type of thinking is counterproductive and never serves a worthwhile purpose.

Black Cotton

The Harvesting of Our Youth

Rev. Al Sharpton

"I think when you look at the lack of diversity in the newsrooms, when you look at the lack of diversity from the editors and those in power, then you see them as automatically dismissive of anything that is not like them, which is white males," (Glover, 2003)

The Harvesting of Our Youth

To The Media

Dear Members of the Media:

    Although the days of smoke rooms filled with typewriters and interviews in bars with mobsters and politicians to get the real story have been replaced with computers and the almighty Internet, we still need reporters who seek the truth behind the lie. Most members of the American media are still genuinely interested in the truth and believe that the public has a right to know; however, we so often see truth placed on the back burners and sacrificed for ratings. Evidence of this is all over TV these days. How is it possible that Brittney Spears is more important than children living in a gang war zone in inner-city Chicago? How is it possible that of the 2,000,000 inmates in America, 50%

of them are blacks and the media has not aggressively investigated the situation? How is it possible for the so-called right-to-life advocates to get press to voice their opinions, but are never questioned about why the church is not shouting to high heaven concerning police brutality, racial profiling, and the right to life for children who live in America's ghettos?

I applaud reporters who push the envelope and stand up for what is right. We need more of that kind of reporting and less capitulating to the interest of big business and political parties.

What can individual reporters, media organizations, and the general public do, to make your jobs easier? How can we support your efforts to report on stories that can bring light to the injustice suffered by the poor? I ask that you seek to effect social change by exposing the injustice in the criminal justice system and those who benefit from the mass incarceration of America.

Black Cotton

Senator Paul Wellstone

"I do not believe the future will belong to those who are content with the present. The future will belong to those who have passion, and to those grassroots heroes who are willing to make the personal commitment to make our country better. The future will belong to those who believe in the beauty of their dreams." (Wellstone, 1998)

Fact

"Black and Hispanic Americans, and other minority groups as well, are victimized by disproportionate targeting and unfair treatment by police and other front-line law enforcement officials; by racially skewed charging and plea bargaining decisions of prosecutors; by discriminatory sentencing practices; and by the failure of judges, elected officials and other criminal justice policy makers to redress the inequities that become more glaring every day (Weich & Angulo, 2000).

To Congress

Dear Members of Congress:

I am aware that many of you are just as passionate about the issues that this book addresses as I am. I am also aware that there have been efforts made to pass legislation intended to reform our criminal justice system; however, we need a more grassroots and organized effort that will persuade your colleagues to get on board with passing meaningful legislation for the healing and protection of our most vulnerable citizens. This result is achievable with courageous leadership. We need genuine community leaders to step into the deep waters of not-so-popular issues and make the reforming of our criminal justice system as

${\bf B}$lack Cotton

The Harvesting of Our Youth

---

important as the rebuilding of Iraq or protecting the environment. Are not poor children also a natural resource as well? We need you to lead and step out of your political comfort zones and take on these issues. Can we count on you to help us organize and make a real difference in our nation?

The historic election of President Barack Obama is only the beginning of change. We need to wage war on poverty and the systems that support it. We are counting on you!

Black Cotton

The Harvesting of Our Youth

Marian Wright Edelman

Incarceration is becoming the new American apartheid and poor children of color are the fodder. It is time to sound a loud alarm about this threat to American unity and community, act to stop the growing criminalization of children at younger and younger ages, and tackle the unjust treatment of minority youths and adults in the juvenile and adult criminal justice systems with urgency and persistence. The failure to act now will reverse the hard-earned racial and social progress for which Dr. Martin Luther King, Jr., and so many others, died and sacrificed" (Edelman, 2009).

Black Cotton

The Harvesting of Our Youth

Fact

Thirteen percent of all adult black men --
1.4 million -- are disenfranchised,
representing one-third of the total
disenfranchised population and reflecting a
rate of disenfranchisement that is seven
times the national average. Election voting
statistics offer an approximation of the
political importance of black
disenfranchisement: 1.4 million black men
are disenfranchised compared to 4.6
million black men who voted in 1996"
(Human Rights Watch, 2000).

To The
President

Dear Mr. President:

First let me state that I am one of your most loyal supporters. I have not seen such a brilliant and genuine political leader in my lifetime, God bless your presidency.

Mr. President, we need your leadership in this movement to reform our broken criminal justice system. You share many of the same concerns I have expressed in this book. I'm also aware that this text may alarm many, however the message is clear, and I trust you will

Black Cotton

consider ways your administration can move the Black Cotton Agenda forward.

As I listened to your timely and eloquent speeches during the campaign, I thought, "Can he actually make the big changes, or will he receive insurmountable opposition?" I wondered, "Will he truly be able to help the poor without jeopardizing his chances for re-election?" Sir, after all of that thinking and wondering, I have come to the conclusion that God will open the hearts and minds of those you inspire. From this inspiration, leaders will emerge with the courage to take bold steps toward social and economic justice. From rural Mississippi to the south side of Chicago, from impoverished communities in Detroit to the security-barred homes of Compton, we will transform this nation into a place where all Americans have a real chance at achieving their dreams.

In closing, sir, I would like to request that you move quickly as possible towards the structured release of all non-violent drug offenders. These nonviolent offenders have no place in jail. Many of our unjust sentencing laws only rip families and communities apart, this must stop. These nonviolent drug offenders should be released, under a structured plan, into drug treatment programs and or behavior modification programs. This will reunite and heal poor communities instead of tearing them apart. This release process will also create jobs in the private sector as private correctional firms will be forced to change their business models to treatment instead of punishment.

Sir, we are building a national coalition to assist you with making this a reality. The members of the Black Cotton Coalition are a network of individuals both young and old, Christian, Muslim and Jew who are ready to support your efforts to empower all Americans to be involved in her growth toward a more perfect union.

God Bless you Mr. President and God Bless America.

Black Cotton

The Harvesting of Our Youth

Tavis Smiley

"Every time I go behind prison bars, I'm always struck by two things. One, there but for the grace of God go I, and number two, I've tried to stop in my own life saying what I will not do" (Smiley, 2007).

To The Church

Dear Church Leaders:

Early in my work as a community economic development consultant, I made a decision to specialize in working with churches that had the potential to make a significant impact on poor communities. I saw small organizations struggling to keep the lights on, not to mention taking on large projects. Of course there are always exceptions to this rule, because sometimes large things come in small packages, but for the most part it takes larger organizations with significant resources to get things done in communities. I saw the church as the institutions most equipped to confront major social and economic issues in poor communities. While pursuing churches that might be willing to take on the myriad challenges facing the communities they served, I learned very quickly that many of them were not remotely interested. There are basically two types of churches, when it comes to community development, inward churches and outward churches. Inward churches are typically concerned only about what's going on inside the wall of their ministries, and if you are not a tithing member of the ministry, you will probably not get any support from that church beyond an occasional community picnic or clothing closet. They might even sponsor a local school function and donate to the local homeless shelter, but not much more than that. Outward churches, on the other hand, aggressively seek to transform the communities in which they serve. They are engaged in the development of affordable housing, drug treatment programs, job training programs, staffing services, offender re-entry programs, and more. Outward churches see the church as a central place for community transformation.

Which one of these designations would you say your church falls within? Are you an inward or outward church? I trust that all churches interested in this book are outward ministries or, at the very least, seeking to become more outward in their approach to community.

Historically in poor and oppressed communities in America, churches served as the central gathering places and provided basic needs for their communities. I have seen churches that have hundreds of thousands in tithes and offerings and have never attempted to build an affordable house or even provide shelter for the homeless. I often think that charismatic preaching and building mega churches are the only real vision that many of our church leaders have these days.

It is my prayer that if you have found this book, you will be both outraged and inspired to become a part of the solution and adopt the Black Cotton Agenda as part of your outward community economic development efforts.

God bless you.

Black Cotton

William Butler Yates

"It takes more courage to dig deep into the abyss of one's own soul than it takes for a soldier to fight on the battlefield" (West, 2002).

To My Brothers

Dear Brothers:

I greet you in the words of our new movement, Black Cotton. I hope one day to personally hear this response to my greeting, "Growing Tall." In spite of the forces that have historically attempted to hold us back, I encourage you to grow tall in your lives. Grow tall socially by first nurturing and loving your children and wives, learning to build real relationships with each other, so we can unite with one mission, one vision, and one purpose against the forces that would see us dead or behind bars. Grow tall by being responsible for not breaking the law in any way. Grow tall in your

Black Cotton

communities by becoming fathers to the fatherless and supporters to the husbandless. Grow tall by protecting and respecting our elders and correcting and leading the youth. Grow tall economically by getting a better education and opening businesses. Grow tall spiritually by fearing, loving, and serving God.

Finally, brothers, grow tall by going to the streets, churches, schools, jails, and prisons to teach other's brothers how to grow tall as well.

Growing with you,

Vincent D. Lewis

Join The Movement

This book is intended to set a fire that will burn down the walls of injustice in our current criminal justice system while empowering our people to grow tall socially, politically, spiritually and economically. We invite you to join the "Black Cotton Movement" by going to our website and adding your voice to our chorus for justice.

www.blackcotton.org

God Bless.

Black Cotton

The Harvesting of Our Youth

Help Sound the Alarm!

You can help by sponsoring books for current inmates, ex-offenders or for anyone who you think needs to join our movement. Getting books on the inside of prisons is one way we can begin to fight back. We are in a war to save our community and having the right information is critical. Also, we need to prevent young black males from becoming future victims of the system, so be sure to share a copy of this book with the youth.

You can contact the author at: booking@blackcotton.org for personal appearance request. Requests are accepted for your book clubs, community organizations or prison ministry events.

Thank you for joining the fight for justice!

Black Cotton

The Harvesting of Our Youth

Dr. Martin Luther King Jr.

Let freedom ring from the snowcapped Rockies of Colorado!

Let freedom ring from the curvaceous peaks of California!

But not only that; let freedom ring from Stone Mountain of Georgia!

Let freedom ring from Lookout Mountain of Tennessee!

Let freedom ring from every hill and every molehill of Mississippi. From every mountainside, let freedom ring.

(King, 1963)

Works Cited

Drug Policy Alliance. (2002). *Effectiveness of the War on Drugs.*
Retrieved June 18th, 2009, from Drug Alliance Policy:
http://www.drugpolicy.org/library/factsheets/effectivenes/i
ndex.cfm

Mother Jones magazine . (2001, July). *States and Black Incarceration
in America* . Retrieved Dec. 23, 2008, from
Gibbsmagazine.com:http://www.gibbsmagazine.com/blacks
_in_prisons.htm

Administrative Office of the Courts. (2004, April 22). *Report on the
Status of North Carolina's Drug Treatment Courts.* Retrieved
June 15, 2009, from nccourts.org:
http://www.nccourts.org/Citizens/CPrograms/DTC/documen
ts/NDlegRp2004.pdf

Cosby, B. (2007, Oct. 18th). Interview With Bill Cosby. (L. king,
Interviewer)

Bird, J. (2005, June 5th). *Part 1: The largest slave rebellion in U.S. history*. Retrieved Dec. 15th, 2008, from www.johnhorse.com:http://www.johnhorse.com/highlights/ essays/largest.htm

Bond, J. (2007). Remarks of NAACP National Board of Directors Chairman Julian Bond. *98th Annual NAACP Convention*. Detroit .

Brooks, R. L. (1996). *Integration or Separation: A Strategy for Racial Equality*. Cambridge: Harvard University Press .

City of Chicago. (n.d.). *Alternatives to Incarceration in Illinois*. Retrieved Aug. 27, 2009, from chicagometropolis2020.org: http://www.chicagometropolis2020.org/documents/Alterna tivestoIncarcerationPaper.pdf

Cleaver, E. (1998, February 10). The Two Nations of Black America. (H. L. Jr., Interviewer)

Common Sense for Drug Policy . (2008). *Get The Facts*. Retrieved July 10th, 2009, from DrugWarfacts.org: http://www.drugwarfacts.org/cms/

Davis, D. A. (1998, Sept 22nd). Retrieved 2009 10th, June, from Time.com:http://www.time.com/time/community/transcrip ts/chattr092298.html

Deterling, D. (1982). How a Cotton Plant Grows. *Progressive Farmer* .

Dyson, M. E. (2009, Feb. 24). *Commentary: Me and my brother and black AmericaStory Highlights*. Retrieved July 20, 2009, from CNN:http://www.cnn.com/2008/US/07/23/bia.michael.dyson/index.html

Edelman, M. W. (2009, Feb. 6th). *"The Cradle to Prison Pipeline: America's New Apartheid"*. Retrieved July 18th, 2009, from childrensdefense.or http://www.childrensdefense.org/child-research-data-publications/data/marian-wright-edelman-child-watch-column/Cradle-to-prison-pipeline-americas-new-apartheid.html

Engelberg, S. (1986, Oct. 15). Report Links Ex-Senate Aide To Contras. *The New York Times* , p. p. 6.

Farrakhan, L. (1993). *A torchlight for America*. Chicago: FCN Pub. Co.

Feder, D. (2005, June 23). *Gary Webb's "Dark Alliance" Returns to the Internet*. Retrieved June 20th, 2009, from The Narco NewsBulletin:http://www.narconews.com/darkalliance/index.htm

Black Cotton

The Harvesting of Our Youth

Foxworth, R. D. (2007, Nov. 6th). *ALONE AT THE TABLE* . Retrieved July 20th, 2009, from Urbanite: http://www.urbanitebaltimore.com/sub.cfm?issueID=42&sectionID=4&articleID=543

Glover, M. (2003, Aug. 7th). *Al Sharpton Criticizes White Media.* Retrieved 2009 10th, June, from APOnline.org: http://www.encyclopedia.com/doc/1P1-77198830.html

Henderson, W. (2009, April 29th). *Restoring Fairness to Federal Sentencing: Addressing the Crack-Powder Disparity.* Retrieved May 15th, 2009, from civilrights.org: http://www.civilrights.org/advocacy/testimony/henderson-crack.html

Hooker, R. (1996). *The African Diaspora* . Retrieved Dec. 24, 2008, from Slave Rebellions : http://www.wsu.edu:8080/~dee/DIASPORA/REBEL.HTM

Human Rights Watch. (2000). Punishment and Prejudice: Racial Disparities in the War on Drugs. *Human Rights Watch* , Vol. 12, No. 2 (G).

Black Cotton

The Harvesting of Our Youth

Interactive, WGBH. (1998). *The Africans in America*. Retrieved June
10, 2008 , from www.pbs.org:
http://www.pbs.org/wgbh/aia/home.html

Jackson, J. (2000, 08 03). Shadow Convention. Philadelphia, PA, USA.

Lapsansky, E. (n.d.). *Brotherly Love*. Retrieved Aug. 26, 2009, from
Africans in America:
http://www.pbs.org/wgbh/aia/part3/3i3119.html

Lotke, P. W. (2004). *Prisoners of the Census.* Northampton: Prisoners
of the Census: Electoral and Financial Consequences of
Counting Prisoners Where They Go, Not Where They Come
From.

Manza, J., & Uggen, C. (2006). *Locked Out: Felon Disenfranchisement
and American Democracy (.* New York: Oxford Press.

Merritt, J. (2004, May 26th). *The Scam of the California Prison
Guards Union.* Retrieved Dec. 18th, 2008, from
www.talkleft.com:http://www.talkleft.com/story/2004/05/2
6/359/29521

National Center for PTSD . (2008, April 22). *PTSD Fact Sheet.* Retrieved June 20th, 2009, from athealth.com: http://www.athealth.com/Consumer/disorders/ptsdfacts.html

National Commission on Institutions and Alternatives. (2007). *What Every American Should Know About the Criminal Justice System.* Retrieved Jan. 10th, 2009, from stopviolence.com: http://stopviolence.com/cj-knowledge.htm#govt

National Inventors Hall of Fame Foundation, Inc. (2002). *Hall of Fame Inventor Profile.* Retrieved Jan. 10th , 2009, from Invent.org: http://www.invent.org/Hall_Of_Fame/152.html

New Jersey Department of Health and Senior Services. (2007, May 02). *Strategic Plan to Eliminate Health Disparities in NJ, 2007* . Retrieved Aug. 5th, 2008, from Strategic Plan Home Page : http://www.newjersey.gov/health/omh/plan/index.shtml

PBS. (n.d.). *Unatural Causes.* Retrieved Aug. 26, 2009, from When the Bough Breaks: http://www.pbs.org/unnaturalcauses/hour_02.htm

Piette, B. (2005, June 10th). *Wachovia admits slave trade profits.* Retrieved June 15th , 2008, from workers.org: http://www.workers.org/2005/us/wachovia-0616/

*B*lack Cotton

The Harvesting of Our Youth

Drew, R. B. (2006). *The Truth About Concentrated Poverty*. Retrieved July 01, 2009 , from NHI Sheterforce Online: http://www.nhi.org/online/issues/147/concentratedpoverty.html

Ravitch, D. (1998, Aug.). *A New Era in Urban Education?* Retrieved July 20th, 2009, from BROOKINGS: http://www.brookings.edu/papers/1998/08education_ravitch.aspx

Rose, W. L. (1999). *A documentary history of slavery in North America*. Athens and London: University of Georgia Press.

Sabol, W. J. (2008). Bureau of Justice Statistics, Prison Inmates at Midyear2007., (pp. NCJ221944, p. 7, Table 10.). Washington, DC.

Sarin, V. (Director). (2000). *LEFT BEHIND* [Motion Picture].

Scherer, J. A. (1916). *Cotton as a world power; a study in the economic interpretation of history*. New York: Frederick A. Stokes Company.

Black Cotton

The Harvesting of Our Youth

Shah, P. (2005). *MODERN TOUGH ON CRIME MOVEMENT* . Retrieved Aug. 26, 2009, from publiceye.or: http://www.publiceye.org/defendingjustice/con_agendas/toughcrime.html

Shakur, T. (Composer). (2004). Black Cotton. [T. Shakur, Performer]

Smiley, T. (2007, March 30). *Tavis Smiley* . Retrieved July 10th, 2009, from ps.org: http://www.pbs.org/kcet/tavissmiley/archive/200703/20070330_monique.html

Stewart, R. (2002). African American males' reported involvement in the criminal justice system: A descriptive analysis. *Journal of African American Studies* , 55-70.

The Coalition for Jubilee Clemency. (2002, November). Retrieved June 29th, 2009, from cjpf.org: http://cjpf.org/clemency/cjc.html

Uminski, D. J., & Chizek, C. (2008, Feb./ Mar.). *How to Play the Incentives Game*. Retrieved June 9th, 2009, from areadevelopment.com:http://www.areadevelopment.com/taxesIncentives/feb08/howToPlay.shtml

Washington, D. (Director). (2007). *The Great Debaters* [Motion Picture].

Wellstone, S. P. (1998, July 11). *Grass Roots Heroes* . Retrieved 2008 23rd, Dec., from geocities.com: http://www.geocities.com/~demcrat/frame28.html

West, D. C. (2002, May 15th). *essentialschools.org*. Retrieved June 28th, 2009, from CES National WEB: 2009

West, D. C. (Composer). (2001). Sketches of My Culture. [D. C. West, Performer]

X, M. (1965, Feb. 11th). Malcolm X on Racist Violence. London , England .

Yuksel, E. (2001). *Prison as a Prism*. Retrieved Aug. 26, 2009, from yuksel.org: http://www.yuksel.org/e/law/prison.htm

Black Cotton

The Harvesting of Our Youth

www.ingramcontent.com/pod-product-compliance
Lightning Source LLC
Chambersburg PA
CBHW020615270326
41927CB00005B/339